SRA Early Interventions in Reading

EARTHQUAKES:
Making Buildings Stronger

By
Linda Barr

Illustrated by
Kristen Goeters

Columbus, OH

The McGraw·Hill Companies

Photo Credits

Cover, Back Cover ©Roger Ressmeyer/CORBIS.

SRAonline.com

 SRA

Send all inquiries to:
SRA/McGraw-Hill
8787 Orion Place
Columbus, OH 43240-4027

Printed in the United States of America.

ISBN 0-07-604469-6

3 4 5 6 7 8 9 MAL 10 09 08 07 06

Contents

Chapter 1
Earthquake!

"Why is the ground shaking?" Carlos asked.

He was sitting on a blanket with his cousins Hilda and Julia, his grandma, and his grandpa. They were having the nicest picnic at a park.

"It's an earthquake!" his grandma yelled. "Let's get away from these trees."

They rushed to a field.

Carlos lived in Missouri. He hadn't visited California in the longest time; this was his first earthquake. He would remember this visit for a long time!

The ground continued to shake. Carlos thought it would never stop. His grandma was hugging him, Hilda, and Julia tighter and tighter, but he was still scared!

Finally the earthquake was over, and they heard fire trucks. Carlos and his family hurried home, but driving wasn't easy. Some streets and buildings had the biggest cracks he'd ever seen.

A few porches had fallen down. Some people had come outside so nothing could fall on them inside. No one seemed to be hurt.

At last they turned onto his grandparents' street. Hilda yelled, "Your house is all right!"

Carlos was glad about that, but he was also puzzled. Why were some houses all right while others were destroyed? How could the same earthquake crack some buildings and not hurt others?

That night the TV showed pictures of parts of the town that had been hit the nastiest. Again, Carlos saw that other buildings weren't damaged at all.

"Are some buildings stronger than others?" he asked.

"I can explain that," his grandpa said. "First I will tell you about earthquakes. I just need a hard-boiled egg."

Chapter 2
A Whole Lot of Shaking

His grandpa found an egg in the kitchen. He tapped it softly, and the shell cracked.

"Earth is covered with a rocky shell," he explained. "Earth's shell is cracked like this egg, but those cracks are very deep underground. Earth's shell has about twelve main pieces called plates."

"These plates move very slowly," his grandpa told them. "They push against each other."

He held his hands out flat and said, "Imagine my hands are Earth's plates." Then he pushed his hands together harder and harder.

"Watch out! A lot of energy is building up," he said.

Suddenly his grandpa let one hand slide under the other.

"When the plates slide, they move the ground above them," he said. "We call it an earthquake. Some earthquakes are very small. We don't even feel the slightest shake. Others shake the ground really hard, and buildings fall down."

"But why do some buildings fall down and others don't?" Carlos asked.

"Well, do you remember what happened when Julia threw a stone into the pond at the park?" his grandma asked him.

Carlos nodded and said, "The stone made waves that spread out in bigger and bigger circles."

"Earthquakes send out waves too," his grandma said. "These waves are made of energy, not water. The first waves push the ground from side to side, and the next waves push the ground up and down. All this shaking can damage anything built on that ground!"

"But why does shaking damage just some buildings?" Carlos asked.

"We have found ways to keep buildings from falling down," his grandma explained. She was an engineer and helped plan new buildings. "We've learned many things about dealing with earthquakes."

"What's the neatest thing you've learned?" Julia asked.

Chapter 3
Problems, Problems

"First, no building is really 'earthquake proof,'" his grandma said. "A very strong earthquake can damage any building. It can cause any bridge to fall. It can crack any road."

Carlos shook his head and thought about going back to Missouri. He had never felt an earthquake there!

"Still, some buildings are damaged by the smallest quakes. Many of those buildings are made of concrete," his grandma said. "Concrete is like the cement in sidewalks. Concrete makes buildings stronger—and stiffer.

"Earthquakes jerk buildings," she said. "A concrete building can't bend or sway. It just cracks."

Carlos thought about the damaged buildings he had seen. A few of them did look like piles of cement chunks.

"Now builders put long steel rods in the concrete," his grandma said. "The rods make the buildings stronger. Then the buildings can bend just a little without cracking."

"Bending too much can also be a problem," his grandma said. "For example, a wide roof, such as a gym roof, should not bend easily. An earthquake can make a wide roof flop up and down. Then the roof might cave in."

Building in California was not easy!

Hilda said, "What about that office building we saw on TV? It was wood and didn't have a wide roof. It still fell down."

"Its first floor was a garage, which has lots of open space," his grandma said. "The garage couldn't hold up the floors above it."

"Now we make garages stronger," his grandma said. "We also try to build on rock. Rock soaks up some of an earthquake's nastiest energy. If a house is built on soft soil, the soil can turn into liquid in an earthquake!"

Carlos stared at his toes on the floor. Was his grandparents' house built on rock?

Chapter 4
What Works

"We have found more ways to keep buildings from shaking too," his grandma said. "One way is to put layers of rubber and steel under buildings. The quake hits these layers first. The layers soak up some of its unsafe energy. Then the building does not shake so much."

"Some buildings have a special base that slides," his grandma told them.

She drew two buildings and showed what would happen in an earthquake. One unstable building swayed back and forth, but the other building had a sliding base. If an earthquake hit, only the base would sway.

"How do you know what works?" Carlos asked.

"We put instruments in many buildings," his grandma explained. "The instruments tell how much each building moves during an earthquake. We know if the building moves up and down, side to side, or both. After a quake, we check for unfortunate damage."

"We see how well each kind of building does in a quake," his grandma said. "That tells us what works and what's unsuccessful."

Just then, a man on TV said no one else was trapped in any buildings. Still, Carlos saw some workers poking around in the hardest-hit buildings.

"They are trying to find out why each unsteady building cracked or fell," his grandpa said. "That helps us understand what works and what doesn't."

"Well, I'm glad we don't have any earthquakes in Missouri!" Carlos said.

His grandpa smiled and asked, "Have you ever heard of New Madrid?"

Chapter 5
Earthquakes Are Everywhere

"New Madrid is in Missouri. It's south of the town where you live," his grandpa said. "This town had one of our country's biggest earthquakes."

His grandma nodded. "It was really three big quakes. They were in 1811 and 1812. Unbelievably, the first one shook the ground over hundreds of miles."

"That first earthquake rang church bells in Boston," his grandma said. "That's a thousand miles away! It made part of the Mississippi River run backward!"

"The unsafe earthquakes knocked down whole towns," his grandpa said. "Nothing could stand up to earthquakes back then."

Maybe Carlos should stay in California!

"I thought only California had earthquakes," Julia said.

"No, Alaska has the highest number of quakes of all the states," his grandma said. "California has the second-most earthquakes, but many other states have earthquakes too. They are all caused by Earth's unstable plates pushing on one another."

"Will New Madrid ever have another quake?" Carlos asked. "Will it make my town fall down?"

"Actually, earthquakes still do happen near New Madrid. However, people are trying to make sure they aren't unprepared," his grandma said. "They are learning more about Earth's plates in that area."

"Now I remember that we had some earthquake drills at school in the uncomfortable basement," Carlos said. "I had never been in an earthquake before. Now I know why the drills are important!"

Hilda smiled and said, "We have earthquake drills at school all the time." She smiled wider. "Some of them are for real!"

Carlos shook his head. "I have learned more about Missouri by coming to California! I know more about safer buildings now too."

His grandma nodded and gave her grandson a hug. "Maybe you will become an engineer someday. Then you can plan unbreakable buildings that help save people's lives!"